BLACK HOLES

A TRUE BOOK

by
Paul P. Sipiera

Children's Press®
A Division of Grolier Publishing
New York London Hong Kong Sydney
Danbury, Connecticut

A rocky planet orbiting around a pulsar

Reading Consultant
Linda Cornwell
Learning Resource Consultant
Indiana Department of Education

Science Consultant
Samuel Storch
Lecturer,
American Museum-Hayden Planetarium, New York City

Dedication: To all my coworkers at William Rainey Harper College, my home for more than twenty years

Library of Congress Cataloging-in-Publication Data

Sipiera, Paul P.
    Black Holes / by Paul Sipiera.
        p.   cm. — (A true book)
    Includes bibliographical references and index.
    Summary: Explains the nature and formation of the cosmic phenomenon known as a black hole.
    ISBN 0-516-20326-6 (lib.bdg.)   0-516-26162-2 (pbk.)
    1.Black Holes (Astronomy)—Juvenile literature. [1. Black holes (Astronomy). I. Title. II. Series.
QB843.B55.S57 1997
523.8' 875—dc20   96-36149
                                                                        CIP
                                                                        AC

Contents

A supernova (bright spot at bottom right) is an explosion that marks the end of the life of a massive star.

An Amazing Universe

Our universe contains many amazing things. Some stars are so massive that they have short lives before dying in violent explosions. Other stars contain so little mass that they seem to shine forever. Certain galaxies are seen to have giant explosions, while others simply collide. Although many planets orbit stars, most are not like the Earth. Our universe is filled with many unusual and wondrous things.

Perhaps the most mysterious of all cosmic things is a black hole. Most black holes form after a supernova—the explosion of a giant star. During such an explosion, a huge amount of matter is thrown into space. What is

An artist's impression of a supernova as seen from a nearby planetary system

left becomes crushed by gravity into a smaller and smaller object. The remains of the star, now called a "black hole," will seem to disappear from our universe.

An artist's impression of the activity surrounding a black hole

It cannot be seen, because its gravity is so strong that it "pulls" all light into it.

Mass and Gravity

In order to understand a black hole, we must know something about mass and gravity. Mass is the quantity of material that makes up all things. Every object has mass. The mass of an object causes the object to attract other objects. This attraction is

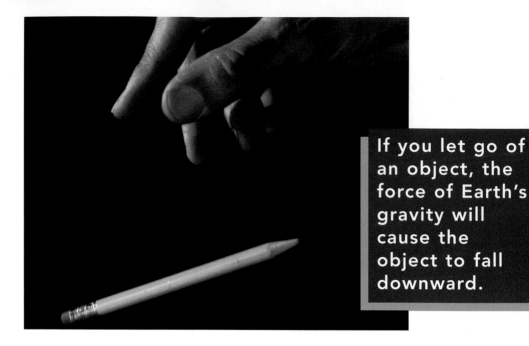

If you let go of an object, the force of Earth's gravity will cause the object to fall downward.

called gravity. Put another way, gravity is the force of attraction between two masses.

Sometimes people confuse mass and weight. Weight is a measure of the force of gravity between an object and the Earth. When you weigh yourself on a scale, what the scale is really telling you is how hard the Earth's gravity is pulling on you. Astronauts in space do not feel this force because they are too far from

When in space, astronauts are weightless because they are far from the Earth and its pull is not as strong.

Earth. They are said to be "weightless," but they still have the same amount of mass as they have always had.

The amount of speed needed to escape the gravity of an object is called an escape velocity. If a rocket moves fast enough to escape Earth's gravity, it has reached its escape velocity. A rocket moving in a low orbit around Earth may be moving at 17,500 miles (28,000 kilometers) per hour.

A rocket needs to achieve great speed to escape the Earth's gravity.

To escape Earth's gravity and go to the Moon, the rocket must move faster than 25,000 miles (40,000 km) per hour, which is the escape velocity from Earth.

Because objects like Jupiter and the Sun are more massive than Earth, they have higher escape velocities. The more massive an object is, the stronger its gravity becomes.

To understand escape velocity, throw a ball straight up into the air. It will leave your hand quite fast, but it will go only so high. This is the force of gravity at work. It pulls your ball back down. If you throw the ball harder, it

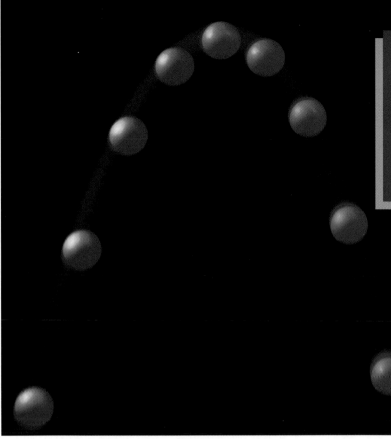

If you throw a ball into the air, it will go only so high before the Earth's gravity pulls it back down.

will go higher. But it will always fall back to the Earth. No baseball player could ever throw a ball fast enough to escape Earth's gravity.

On Deimos You'd Have Quite an Arm!

On Deimos, a tiny moon of Mars, the force of gravity is so low that almost anybody could toss a baseball into orbit around it.

The first person to use mathe-
matics to describe gravity was
Isaac Newton. He discovered
that there is a force that moves
the Moon around the Earth. He
realized that this force explained
the motion of not only the Earth

English physicist Isaac Newton
(1642-1727) (right) discovered that
gravity was the force that kept the
moon in orbit around the Earth.

and Moon, but every object in the universe.

Newton also realized that the force of gravity grows weaker as two objects get farther apart. The opposite is also true. The closer two objects are, the stronger gravity becomes. In this way, Newton's discovery predicted a black hole. If an object can be made very small without losing any mass, it will then have the strongest possible gravity.

A Black Hole

Newton's discovery of gravity provided scientists with the idea of a black hole. In the early 1900s, the work of physicist Albert Einstein made the concept of a black hole even more possible. In studying Einstein's general theory of relativity,

This drawing (above) is an artist's impression of a black hole pulling in material from a companion star. The theories of German-born American physicist Albert Einstein (left) gave support to the idea that black holes exist.

astronomer Karl Schwartzchild
realized that any object could
become a black hole. All it
has to do is to become small
enough and dense enough.

If the Earth could be
squeezed into a ball a half
inch (1.2 centimeters) across,
it would become a black hole.
It would have enough gravity
to cause light to return to
itself. A person would have to
travel faster than the speed of
light to escape its pull.

How a Black Hole Forms

Most astronomers believe that a black hole forms from the death of a giant star. When a star that has more than three times the mass of the Sun explodes, it becomes a super-nova. Such a star throws off much of its mass and energy. A great cloud of matter is

What a supernova may look like up close

blown into space. For a short period of time, the star can give off as much energy as an entire galaxy.

Once this energy and matter is gone, gravity causes the core of the star to shrink.

The top photograph shows an expanding gas cloud from a supernova. The bottom photographs show a star before (left) and after (right) it exploded into a supernova.

The crushing weight of matter falling inward from all sides compresses the dying star into a tight, extremely dense mass. When the star shrinks to 60 miles (100 km) in diameter or less, it is called a neutron star.

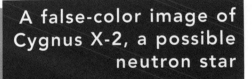

A false-color image of Cygnus X-2, a possible neutron star

A neutron star is so dense that one teaspoon of its material would weigh 100 million tons on Earth! The gravity of a neutron star is so

The tremendous gravity of a neutron star (at right) pulls matter away from a nearby companion star.

strong that it pulls almost all of its energy back to the star. If a companion star is close enough, matter will be pulled from it into the neutron star.

The only energy that escapes from a neutron star comes from the north and south magnetic poles. When this happens, the star is called a pulsar. If the collapse process continues, the pulsar will eventually become a black hole.

However, black holes may not always come from single stars. Astronomers believe that most large galaxies have a giant black hole at their center. The giant black hole pulls

An artist's impression of what a galactic black hole might look like

In this X-ray image of the center of our galaxy, the bright spots are thought to be X rays—energy in the form of radiation—being released by a massive black hole.

in more and more stars. As it does, it becomes more massive, and its gravity becomes more powerful. Astronomers think there is a giant black hole "eating out" the center of our own Milky Way galaxy.

29

How Would a Black Hole Look?

Scientists have never seen a black hole. But they do have a good idea of what one looks like. Imagine a black ball in space. It is not very large. Inside it you would see nothing. The surface of this ball would be called the

This diagram of a black hole shows what happens to light coming near it. The five white lines are light rays. The light ray that comes closest to the black hole gets drawn in by the black hole's intense gravity. The "edge" of the ball is the event horizon. The tiny black dot in the center is the singularity.

event horizon. This is the place from which light can no longer escape.

Deep inside the black hole we would come to its center. This is called the singularity. Here all things disappear from our universe as we know them.

The distance between the event horizon and singularity is called the Schwartzchild radius. This measures the actual size of a black hole.

Where Are Black Holes Found?

It is impossible to see a black hole, since one would be looking for a tiny black ball against the blackness of space. Instead, astronomers use clues to find black holes without actually seeing them. They observe how a black hole may affect a nearby star or gas cloud.

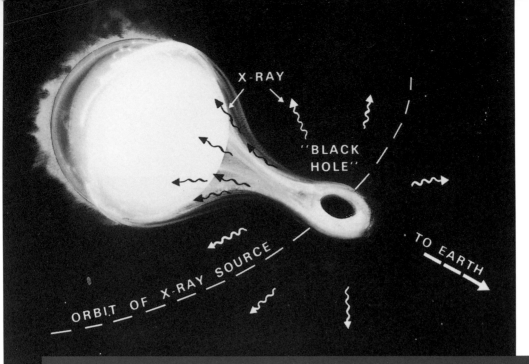

X-RAY

"BLACK HOLE"

TO EARTH

ORBIT OF X-RAY SOURCE

This is a diagram of the black hole discovered in the constellation Cygnus the Swan. As the black hole pulled matter from a nearby star (the white ball), it released energy in the form of X rays. These X rays were what told scientists that a black hole was there. The black hole itself was invisible.

The first possible discovery of a black hole was made by a satellite searching for X rays— extremely tiny high-energy par- ticles—in space. The satellite was looking in the constellation of Cygnus the Swan when it found X rays that seemed to be coming from a star. This was puzzling, because most stars are not hot enough to emit large amounts of X rays.

Black holes, however, do emit X rays. As matter from a nearby star falls into a black hole, it is converted into energy in the form of high temperatures. This energy is released from the black hole as X rays. On closer study, the X rays

The Accretion Disk

Although black holes appear black, most are believed to be surrounded by a bright disk of energy. A black hole pulls in material, rips it apart, and releases huge amounts of energy. As long as a black hole consumes matter, it will have this bright disk around it.

found by the satellite were shown to have been coming from a point very close to the star. This made a strong case for a black hole.

Since the 1970s, astronomers have found several possible black holes. Perhaps the best example lies in the heart of the galaxy called M87. A huge blast of matter and energy has been observed coming from its center. This may be because there are so many stars crowded there. A giant black hole

The core of galaxy M87

could be pulling in what it left behind after blowing the stars apart. Such a giant black hole could be more than 3 billion times the mass of the Sun. It could be the most powerful object in the universe!

Strange Things Would Happen

If you got close to a black hole, strange things would happen. As you got near one, it would slowly pull you, just as if you were approaching any other large body in space. After a while, you would feel yourself moving faster and

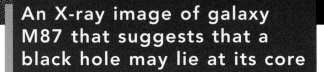

An X-ray image of galaxy M87 that suggests that a black hole may lie at its core

faster. By the time you would be moving as fast as light, you would be at the event horizon of the black hole. That is, if you could survive the trip.

If you were falling head first into a black hole, you would look very strange. Your head would get stretched out and become much farther from your feet. You would get taller, but would become very skinny. Why? Since the force of gravity between two objects increases as they come closer together, gravity would be pulling on your head more strongly than on your feet.

A Final Frontier

An astronomer can peer through a telescope and see across both space and time. It takes so long for the light from a distant galaxy to reach us that we see the galaxy as it was long ago, not as it is today.

The study of black holes includes both astronomy and physics. Scientists use astronomy to help discover black holes, and physics to understand them. But there are many unanswered questions about black holes. Since it is impossible to see what happens inside of black holes, they are still very much a mystery.

To Find Out More

Here are some additional resources to help you learn more about black holes:

 **Books**

Asimov, Isaac. **Mysteries of Deep Space: Blackholes, Pulsars, and Quasars.** Gareth Stevens, 1994.

Asimov, Isaac. **How Did We Find Out About Black Holes?** Walker & Company, 1978.

Berger, Melvin. **Quasars, Pulsars, and Black Holes in Space.** Putnams' Sons, 1977.

Preston, Richard. **First Light: The Search for the Edge of the Universe.** Penguin, 1987.

Sipiera, Paul P. **Galaxies.** Children's Press, 1997.

Sipiera, Paul P. **Stars.** Children's Press, 1997.

Organizations

Astronomical Society of the Pacific
1290 24th Avenue
San Francisco, CA 94122
http://www.physics.sfsu.edu/asp

Junior Astronomical Society
58 Vaughan Gardens
Ilford Essex IG1 3PD
England

The Planetary Society
5 North Catalina Avenue
Pasadena, CA 91106
email: *tps.lc@genie.geis.com*

Online Sites

Astronet
http://www.xs4all.nl/~carlkop/astroeng.html

Exploring Our Solar System—and Beyond
http://www.reston.com/astro/explore.html

The Planetary Studies Foundation
http://homepage.interaccess.com/~jpatpsf/>.

Important Words

astronomer scientist who studies the stars, planets, and other heavenly bodies

event horizon the surface of a black hole

galaxy billions of stars revolving around a common center of gravity

neutron particle found in the nucleus of most atoms; it has no electrical charge

neutron star star made almost entirely of closely packed neutrons; it can form after a supernova explosion causes a massive star to collapse

Schwartzchild radius the distance between singularity and the event horizon of a black hole

singularity the center of mass of a black hole, where gravity is so strong that the mass has been crushed to a ball with no diameter at all

supernova explosion at the end of a massive star's lifetime that leaves a debris cloud and a dense core that may become a neutron star

Index

Meet the Author

Paul P. Sipiera is a professor of geology and astronomy at William Rainey Harper College in Palatine, Illinois. His main area of research is meteorites. When he is not studying science, he can be found working on his farm in Galena, Illinois, with his wife, Diane, and their two daughters Andrea and Paula Frances.

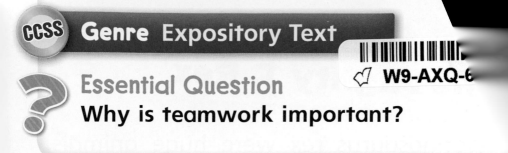

☑ **W9-AXQ-6**

Digging for
SUE

by Susan Evento

he Mighty T. Rex

Tyrannosaurus rex were huge animals. They walked on two legs. They once ruled the earth. That was millions of years ago. How do we know this?

We know this from scientific studies of T. rex **fossils**. An important discovery of T. rex fossils took place in 1990. It led to more information about them.

Tyrannosaurus rex means "king of the tyrant lizards."

In 1990, Sue Hendrickson was part of an exploration. Her team was in South Dakota. They were looking for fossils. One day, Sue walked to some nearby cliffs.

She saw a few small bones on the ground. She saw some huge bones stuck in a cliff. Sue guessed that the bones had probably belonged to a T. rex.

STOP AND CHECK

How do we know about T. rex that lived millions of years ago?

Sue and other fossil hunters started to dig. They used picks and shovels. It took five days of teamwork. But at last they reached the bones.

Fossil hunters may spend hours searching for pieces of bone.

Sue's large jaw held sharp
teeth that were 12 inches long.

Then Sue's team had to work more
carefully. They used smaller tools.
They found many bones. The skull
was about five feet long! The
hunters named this T. rex *Sue*. They
named her for Sue Hendrickson.

The diggers took photographs. They numbered the bones. They wrote notes about them. Some bones were mixed up. Many were just where they were millions of years ago. A few were missing.

Diggers need to work carefully to uncover bones.

The diggers kept some rock around the bones. That way, the bones wouldn't break. They covered the fossils with cloth. It was soaked in plaster. When the plaster dried, it would protect the bones.

People fought over the rights to Sue's bones. Finally, Sue's bones found a home. It was the Field Museum in Chicago.

The plaster is like a cast people wear on a broken bone.

STOP AND CHECK

What steps did people follow to dig up Sue?

7

Chapter 3

At the Museum

Sue's skull took over 3,000 hours to clean.

People at the museum wanted to show off these bones. They had to prepare them first. More than 250 bones had to be cleaned and studied. First, workers removed the plaster. Then, they removed the rock around the bones.

The team used a **CT scanner.** This let them see inside Sue's bones. Her skull wouldn't fit in the scanner. The team sent it to a place where they scan airplane parts for problems!

This is what the scan of Sue's skull looked like.

Putting Sue back together was hard. First, the team fixed cracks in the bones with glue. They used a material like modeling clay. This helped them repair missing parts of bones. They made models of the missing bones.

Putting Sue's bones together was like doing a big puzzle.

The workers made casts of each bone. Copies of Sue's **skeleton** could then be shown in other places. Then they had to put all the pieces together. That was another hard job.

It can take thousands of hours to get a skeleton ready to show.

The workers needed a special frame to hold up the bones. But Sue's skull was too heavy. It could not be placed on top. So they made a lighter plastic cast of it. They placed the real skull in a special case.

Sue's skull is large and hard to lift.

We know that T. rex had small, strong arms. Huge arm muscles left marks on Sue's arm bones. The scans showed something else, too. Sue had an amazing sense of smell!

We also learned that Sue was about 41 feet long. She stood about 12 feet high from the hip. She weighed about 9 tons. She died when she was about 28 years old.

Some bones of a T. rex and a bird look very much alike.

dinosaur

bird

Sue was finally standing tall at the museum.

Millions of people have now visited Sue. She is the largest T. rex ever found. Her fossils are the most complete. They are in the best shape.

As a result of finding new bones, we learn more about dinosaurs. Studying fossils helps us understand the past. They show us how animals have changed over time.

STOP AND CHECK

What did the museum workers do to get Sue ready to show?

Respond to Reading

Summarize

Use details to
help you summarize
Digging for Sue.

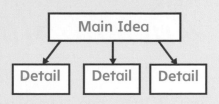

Text Evidence

1. How do you know *Digging for Sue* is expository text? Genre

2. What is the main idea on page 2? Main Idea and Key Details

3. Use what you know about Greek roots to figure out the meaning of *dinosaur* on page 14. Greek and Latin Roots

4. Write about what fossil hunters do to prepare bones. Write About Reading

Compare Texts

Read about how people who explore work as a team.

Ancient Ship Discovered!

In 2010, an ancient ship was uncovered in New York City. A machine was digging at a new building site. Then it hit something hard.

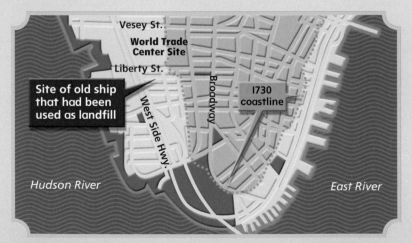

Vesey St.

World Trade Center Site

Liberty St.

Site of old ship that had been used as landfill

West Side Hwy.

Broadway

1730 coastline

Hudson River

East River

Workers found the ship 20 feet underground.

Scientists recorded what they found at the site.

The machine had hit the wooden ship. Scientists hurried to the site. They wanted to dig up the ship. They needed to do it right away. Otherwise, the air would destroy the wood.

Scientists studied a coin found on the ship.

Scientists studied rings in the wood to learn about the age of the ship. They think it was built between 1770 and 1780. Hopefully, more secrets of this ship will be discovered!

Make Connections
Why do people work as a team?
Essential Question

How did the scientists in both stories protect the things they found? Text to Text

Glossary

CT scanner *(SEE TEE SKAN-ur)* machine that takes pictures and lets doctors look inside bodies *(page 9)*

fossils *(FOS-uhlz)* hardened remains of animals or plants that lived long ago *(page 2)*

skeleton *(SKEL-uh-tuhn)* frame that supports and protects the body of an animal *(page 11)*

Index

Focus on Science

Purpose To find out how teamwork helps you explore

What to Do

Step 1 Think about a time when you worked with a team to explore something.

Step 2 Create a chart like this one.

Team Members	What We Did

Conclusion Share your chart with a partner. Talk about how each person helped the team. What did you learn?

20